THE
VINTAGE DOG
BIRTHDAY BOOK

- THE BEAGLE HOUND -

© Vintage Dog Books 2011
This book is copyright and may not be
reproduced or copied in any way without
the express permission of the publisher in writing

British Library Cataloguing-in-Publication Data
A catalogue record for this book is available from
the British Library

VDB

www.vintagedogbooks.com

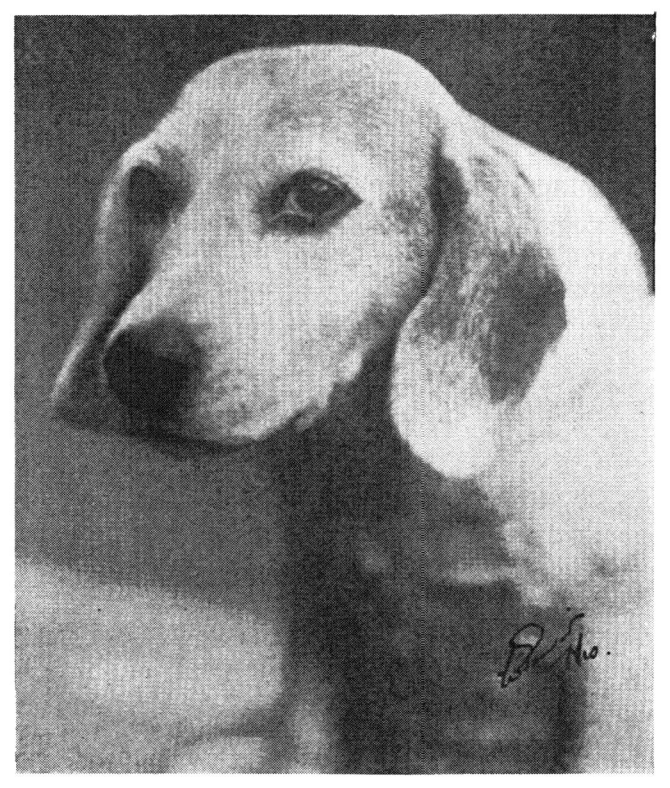

THE BEAGLE CH. MELODY OF REYNALTON

THE BEAGLE   A "REYNALTON" PUPPY

JANUARY

For love, that comes wherever life and sense
Are given by God, in thee was most intense;
A chain of heart, a feeling of the mind,
A tender sympathy, which did thee bind
Not only to us men, but to thy kind;
Yea, for thy fellow brutes in thee we saw
A soul of love, love's intellectual law;
Hence, if we wept, it was not done in shame,
Our tears from passion and from reason came;
And therefore shalt thou be an honoured name

WORDSWORTH. Tribute to a Dog

JANUARY 01

MY lord Archbishop, may I come in with my dog?
TENNYSON. *Becket*, Act i., scene iv.

JANUARY 02

IF I can be as good a brute as my dog here...
      I shall be very well content.
KINGSLEY. *Hypatia*

JANUARY 03

POOR dog! He was faithful and kind to be sure,
And constantly loved me; although I was poor.
CAMPBELL. *Poor Dog Tray.*

JANUARY 04

ASK my dog: if he say "aye," it wilt;
If he say "no," it wilt.
If he say nothing, and shake his tail, it will.
SHAKESPEARE. *Two Gentlemen of Verona, ii. 5.*

JANUARY 05

WHAT the devil do you come between me and my dog for?
DICKENS. *Oliver Twist.*

JANUARY 06

CALLS to the few tired dogs that yet remain:
Blanch, Swift, and Music, noblest of their kind.
WORDSWORTH. *Hart-Leap Well.*

JANUARY 07

GOOD dog Tray is happy now;
He has no time to say "Bow-wow!"
STRUWELPETER. *Naughty Frederick.*

JANUARY 08

MY dog shall mortify the pride of man's superior breed.
COWPER. *The Dog and the Water-Lily.*

H. L. Kreuder's, Nanuet, N. Y.
FRANK FOREST.

JANUARY 09

BUT if I be I, as I suppose I be;
Then I've a little dog at home, and he knows me.
Old Ballad.

JANUARY 10

SIR, he is a good dog, and a fair dog;
Can there be more said; he is good and fair.
SHAKESPEARE. *Merry Wives of Windsor, i. I*

JANUARY 11

"TWO heads are better than one," quoth the
woman when she took her dog to market
with her.
Old Proverb.

JANUARY 12

A SLAUGHTERMAN'S tulip-eared puppy is as
liable to engage one's liking as his chuckle-
headed master.
T. HOOD.

JANUARY 13

MY spaniel, prettiest of his race,
And high in pedigree
COWPER. *The Dog and the Water-Lily*

JANUARY 14

A TRAVELLER, by the faithful hound,
Half-buried in the snow, was found.
LONGFELLOW. *Excelsior*

JANUARY 15

AND God lives in you too – and all your kind.
Yes, good dog, you king of beasts, I see it in
your eyes.
DU MAURIER. *Trilby.*

JANUARY 16

… I HAVE dogs, my lord,
Will rouse the proudest panther in the chase
And climb the highest promontory rock.
SHAKESPEARE. *Titus Andronicus, ii. 2.*

JANUARY 17

YOU must thank my teacher, the dog – not me.
KINGSLEY. *Hypatia.*

JANUARY 18

THERE was speech in their dumbness,
language in their very gesture.
SHAKESPEARE. *Winter's Tale, v. 3.*

JANUARY 19

THE hindmost dog may catch the hare.
Old Proverb.

JANUARY 20

THE sport may be lost by a moment's delay,
So whip up the puppies and scurry away.
KINGSLEY. *The Find.*

Mr. A. H. Higginson's (Middlesex Beagles, So. Lincoln, Mass.)
CHAMPION "FIDDLER"

JANUARY 21

THY wit is as quick as the greyhound's
mouth – it catches.
SHAKESPEARE. *Much Ado about Nothing, v. 2*

JANUARY 22

HE'D make a fortin; on the stage, that dog
would, and revive the drama.
DICKENS. *Oliver Twist.*

JANUARY 23

ALWAYS give your dog, like your wife, their
own way. It saves trouble, as they are
sure to get it in the end.
R. J. LLOYD PRICE. *Dog's Tales.*

JANUARY 24

UNG roy, ung loy, ung chien.
Old Motto.

Oh spare the dog – it saved my father.
KINGSLEY. *Hypatia.*

JANUARY 25

I AM his Highness' dog at Kew;
Pray tell me, sir, whose dog are you?
POPE. *A collar inscription.*

JANUARY 26

A LIVING dog is better than a dead lion.
Eccl. ix. 4.

JANUARY 27

DIDST thou think that I should be faithless
and forsake thee – I, a dog?
OUIDA. *Dog of Flanders.*

JANUARY 28

I THINK the tenderness, chivalry, fidelity, and
prudence of that dog would make a fair
share of virtue for any human being.
R. J. LLOYD PRICE. *Dog's Tales*

JANUARY 29

THOU callest me "a dog" without a cause;
But since I am a dog – beware my fangs.
SHAKESPEARE. *Merchant of Venice, iii. 3.*

JANUARY 30

FOUR dogs, each different breed;
Distinguished, two for scent, and two speed.
WORDSWORTH. *A Dog's Tragedy.*

JANUARY 31

I HAVE all my life had a sympathy for mongrel,
ungainly dogs, who are nobody's pets.
GEORGE ELIOT. *Scenes from Clerical Life.*

'Tis a good dog can catch anything.
Proverb.

Mr. W. N. Crofton's (Calmoor Croft, Totton, Hampshire, Eng.) Pocket or Basket Beagle
"CALMOOR TRAVELER"

FEBRUARY

But the poor dog, in life the firmest friend,
The first to welcome, foremost to defend.
Whose honest heart is still his master's own,
Who labours, fights, lives, breathes for him alone,
Unhonoured falls; unnoticed all his worth,
Denied in heaven, the love he held on earth.
While man, vile insect, hopes to be forgiven,
And claims himself a sole, exclusive Heaven.

BYRON. To a Dog.

FEBRUARY 01

BETTER thy dog than thee. . . . Poor beast!
Poor beast! Set him down. I will bind
up his wounds with my napkin. Give
him a bone.
TENNYSON. *Becket.*

FEBRUARY 02

BEHIND them followed the watch-dog,
Patient, full of importance, and grand in the
pride of his instinct,
Walking from side to side with a lordly air,
and superbly waving his bushy tail.
LONGFELLOW. *Evangeline.*

FEBRUARY 03

BUT of *thee* it shall be said,
This dog watched beside a bed,
Day and night unweary. . . .
E. B. BROWNING. *To my Dog.*

FEBRUARY 04

HE payeth best who loveth best
All things both great and small.
COLERIDGE. *Ancient Mariner*

FEBRUARY 05

HUNTSMAN, I charge thee, tender well my
hounds. . . .
Tomorrow I intend to hunt again.
SHAKESPEARE. *Taming of the Shrew, i.*

FEBRUARY 06

AND as for dogges; Dr. Caynes, a learned
Phisition and a good man, wrote a treatise
of them, and Scriptur itself hath vouch-
safed to commend Tobias Dogge.
HARINGTON. 1591

FEBRUARY 07

A SMALL old Spaniel, which had been Don José's
His father, whom he loved as ye may think,
For on such things the memory reposes
With tenderness.
BYRON. *Don Juan*

FEBRUARY 08

THE old man shall not be deprived of his
faithful dog. I would I had any creature,
were it only a dog, that followed me
because it loved me, not for what it could
make of me.
SCOTT. *Woodstock.*

MRS. OUGHTON-GILES'S POCKET-BEAGLE BENEDICT OF RADNAGE

FEBRUARY 09

HE was a gash an' faithfu' tyke
As ever lap a sheugh or dyke;
His honest, sonsie, bawsn't face,
Aye gat him friends in ika place.
BURNS. *The Twa Dogs*.

FEBRUARY 10

WITH two brave sheep-dogs tried in many a storm,
The one of an inestimable worth,
Made all their household.
WORDWORTH. *Michael*.

FEBRUARY 11

AND I am recompensed, and deem the toils
Of poetry not lost, if verse of mine
May stand between an animal and woe
And teach one tyrant pity for his drudge.
COWPER. *The Task, Book vi*.

FEBRUARY 12

. . . THE wise old hound,
Regardless of the frolic pack, attends
His master's side, or slumbers at his ease
Beneath the bending shade.
SOMERVILLE.

FEBRUARY 13

I WOULD not lose the dog for twenty pounds.
SHAKESPEARE. *Taming of the Shrew, Act i.*

FEBRUARY 14

QUIET, Vixen! You're like the rest of the women
— always putting in your word before you
know why.
GEORGE ELLIOT. *Adam Bede*

FEBRUARY 15

POOR beastie; he's some value, surely, I' God's
sight.
OUIDA. *Puck.*

FEBRUARY 16

IS it not enough to have nine blind puppies at
my back, and an old brute at my heels who
will persist in saving my life.
KINGSLEY. *Hypatia.*

FEBRUARY 17

LIKE angry dogs that snarl at first, and then
display their teeth.
T. HOOD. *The Sea-Spell.*

CHIEN qui abbaye, ne mord pas.
Old Proverb.

FEBRUARY 18

MY heart is great; but it must break with
silence.
SHAKESPEARE. *Richard II., ii. I.*

AY, ay, let the dog have the best.
OUIDA. *Dog of Flanders.*

FEBRUARY 19

A HUGE nondescript sort of a dog, built up of
every breed in France, with the virtues of
all and the vices of none.
DU MAURIER. *Trilby.*

FEBRUARY 20

FOR my part I do wish thou wert a dog
That I might love thee.
SHAKESPEARE. *Timon of Athens, iv. 3.*

From photo by The Kitchener Portrait Co., New Bond Street

MRS. OUGHTON-GILES'S POCKET-BEAGLE DOT 96

FEBRUARY 21

A Pet – a favourite pug – whose squat figure,
black muzzle, and tortuosity of tail that
curled like a head of celery in a salad bowl,
bespoke his Dutch extraction.
Ingoldsby Legends. *Spectre of Tappington.*

FEBRUARY 22

WHEN Peggy's dog her arms imprison,
I often wish my lot was hisn.
T. HOOD. *Huggins and Duggins.*

FEBRUARY 23

I COULDN'T have any other dog but Jip – it
would be so unkind. Besides I couldn't
be such friends with any other dog but
Jip, because he wouldn't have known me
before I was married.
DICKENS. *David Copperfield.*

FEBRUARY 24

I ONCE had a hound, a right good hound,
   A hound both fleet and strong;
He ate my board, and slept by my bed,
   And ran with me, all day long.
KINGSLEY. *Saint's Tragedy.*

FEBRUARY 25

AS true a dog as ever fought at head.
SHAKESPEARE. *Titus Andronicus,*
Act v. scene i.

CANE vaccio non baia indarno.
Italian Proverb.

FEBRUARY 26

No sycophant, although of Spaniel race,
And though no hound, a martyr to the chase.
COWPER. *Epitaph on Top, the Dog.*

FEBRUARY 27

ALONE with that his faithful dog,
Then old, beside him lying at his feet.
WORDSWORTH. *Michael.*

FEBRUARY 28

HIS breast was white, his towzie back
Weel clad wi' coat of glossy black;
His gawnie tail, wi' upward curl,
Hung o'er his hurdies wi' a swirl.
BURNS. *The Twa Dogs.*

FEBRUARY 29

TIME, stern huntsman, who can balk,
Staunch as hound, and fleet as hawk.
SCOTT. *Hunting Song.*

NOTES

FIG. 50.—MR. C. CANDY'S 14IN. BEAGLE LOFTY.

MARCH

Aye, sir, that's a pity, begging your pardon . . . it's a great pity that; beast or body, education should aye be minded. I have six terriers at hame, forbye twa couple of slow hunas, five grews, and a wheen other dogs. There's auld Pepper and auld Mustard, and young Pepper and young Mustard, and little Pepper and little Mustard. I had them a' regularly entered, first in rottens, then wi' stots or weasels, and then wi' the tods and brocks, and now they fear naething that ever cam wi' a hairy skin on't.

SCOTT. Guy Mannering.

MARCH 01

. . . I REMEMBERED then
Thy faithful fondness; for not mean the joy
I felt from they dumb welcome.
SOUTHEY. *On the Death of a Favourite Spaniel.*

MARCH 02

IN truth he was a peerless hound.
SPENSER. *Gelert.*

QUI aime Jean, aime son Chien.
French Proverb.

MARCH 03

IT was a litter – a litter of five,
Four were drowned, and one left alive.
He was thought worthy alone to survive.
Ingoldsby Legends. Bagman's Dog.

MARCH 04

GIVE to dogs what though wouldst deny to men.
SHAKESPEARE. *Timon of Athens, iv. 3.*

LITTLE dogs start the hare, but great ones catch it.
Old Proverb.

MARCH 05

HE was not a big dog when I bought him, but
just a little ball of orange-tawny fluff that I
could carry with one hand. His power
of affection increased with his weight.
DU MAURIER. *Trilby.*

MARCH 06

BELIEVE me, friend Latimer, I would as soon
expose my faithful household dog to a
vain combat with a herd of wolves.
SCOTT. *Redgauntlet.*

MARCH 07

SHAGGY, and lean, and shrewd, with pointed ears,
And tail cropped short; half lurcher and half cur.
His dog attends him!
COWPER. *The Task, Book v.*

MARCH 08

THE tither was a ploughman's collie,
A rhyming, ranting, raving billie.
BURNS. *The Twa Dogs.*

FIG. 51.—MR. WALTER CROFTON'S 10IN. BEAGLE COLONIST.

MARCH 09

POOR dog, he was faithful and kind to be sure,
He constantly loved me, although I was poor;
When sour-looking folk sent me heartless away,
I had always a friend in my poor dog Tray.
CAMPBELL.

MARCH 10

THE little dogs and all,
Tray, Blanche, and Sweetheart – see, they bark
at me.
SHAKESPEARE. *King Lear, Act. iii. Scene vi.*

MARCH 11

A BONNY terrier that, sir, and a fell child at
the vermin, I warrant him – that is, if he's
been well entered, for it a' lies i' that.
SCOTT. *Guy Mannering.*

MARCH 12

A TERRIER, too, that once had been a Briton's,
Who, dying on the coast of Ithica,
The peasants gave the poor dumb thing a pittance.
BYRON. *Don Juan.*

MARCH 13

DOGS think a great deal; when people believe
us asleep nine times out of ten we are
meditating.
OUIDA. *Puck.*

MARCH 14

THE wakeful bloodhound rose, and shook his
hide,
But his sagacious eye an inmate owns.
KEATS. *Eve of S. Agnes.*

MARCH 15

THIS dog only, waited on,
Knowing that when light is gone,
Love remains for shining.
E. B. BROWNING. *To Flush, my Dog.*

MARCH 16

REGENT of flocks was he when the shepherd
slept; their protector
When from the forest at night, through the
starry silence, the wolves howled.
LONGFELLOW. *Evangeline.*

MARCH 17

WHO misuses a dog would misuse a child . . .
they cannot speak for themselves. . . . God
help him!
TENNYSON. *Becket.*

MARCH 18

AND . . . well, the dog was game.
BRET HARTE. *The Hawk's Nest.*

FOREMOST . . . whatever dog was there!
MARY RUSSELL MITFORD.

MARCH 19

EACH dog barks in his own yard.
R. KIPLING. *Jungle Book.*

SAE that the hound him lovit sae
That he will part nae wise him frae.
BARBOUR. *Bruce and the Bloodhound.*

MARCH 20

AND with a courtly grin the fawning hound
Salutes thee cowering.
SOMERVILLE. *The Chase.*

A Group of Leyswood Beagles.

MARCH 21

DOGS gnaw their bones because they cannot swallow them.
Italian Proverb.

MARCH 22

A TAME cheater, i' faith;
You may stroke him as gently as a puppy greyhound.
SHAKESPEARE. *Henry IV., ii. 4.*

MARCH 23

YOUR faithful soldiers . . . follow you like dogs, fight for you like dogs, and have the grave of a dog on the spot where they happen to fall.
SCOTT. *Woodstock.*

MARCH 24

A GOOD dog deserves a good home.
Old Proverb.

MARCH 25

HOW in his mid-career, the setter, struck
Stiff, by the tainted gale, with open nose
Outstretched, and finely sensible . . .
THOMPSON.

MARCH 26

TWO wifies in one house,
Two catties and one mouse,
Two doggies and one bone,
Never did agree in one.
UNKNOWN.

MARCH 27

EVEN a wise man may become attached to
a dog.
GOETHE.

MARCH 28

THE dog who barks loudest is not always the
best watcher.
DOWNEY.

MARCH 29

THEY watch to hear the bloodhound baying,
They watch to hear the war-horn braying.
SCOTT, *Lay of the Last Minstrel.*

MARCH 30

A DOG in office, set to bark
All beggars from his door!
T. HOOD. *Ode to H. Bodkin.*

MARCH 31

LITTLE Flo, a tiny spaniel of the Blenheim
breed, bounced out from beneath a sofa
and began to bark at . . . his pantaloons!
Ingoldsby Legends. Spectre of Tappington.

POCKET BEAGLE CHEERFUL OF RODNANCE (Property of Mrs OUGHTON GILES).

APRIL

Near this spot
Are deposited the remains of one
Who possessed Beauty without Vanity,
Strength without Insolence,
Courage without Ferocity,
And all the Virtues of Man without
his Vices.
This Praise, which would be unmeaning
Flattery
If inscribed over human ashes,
Is but a just tribute to the Memory
of a Dog.

BYRON. Epitaph.

APRIL 01

REMEMBEREST thou my greyhound true?
O'er holt and hill there never flew,
From slip or leash there never sprang
More fleet of foot, or sure of fang.
SCOTT. *Marmion.*

APRIL 02

BY all beloved and loving all,
My Marmion! Favourite of the hall!
MARY RUSSELL MITFORD.

APRIL 03

QUAND un chien se noye, chacun lui offer a boire.
French Proverb.

APRIL 04

NOW let your nose be as keen as beagles,
Your steps as swift as greyhounds.
SHELLEY. *Oedipus Tyrannus.*

APRIL 05

THE dog had watched about the spot, or by his
master's side.
How nourished here, through such long time,
He knows, who gave that love sublime.
WORDSWORTH. *Fidelity.*

APRIL 06

THE watch-dog's voice, that bayed the whispering
wind!
GOLDSMITH.

APRIL 07

HE listens for his trusty hounds.
SCOTT. *The Wild Huntsman.*

APRIL 08

A MASTIFF of true English blood
Loved fighting better than his food.
When dogs are snarling for a bone
He longed to make the war his own,
And often found (where two contend)
To interpose obtained his end.
GAY. *Meddling Mastiff.*

ORPHEUS
Painting by Castiglioni, a famous Italian artist, painted about 1650

APRIL 09

THE dog is not of mountain breed;
Its motions, too, are wild and shy.
WORDWORTH. *Fidelity.*

APRIL 10

OH! . . . to be like you, good dog . . . and
secrete love and goodwill, from morn till
night – from night till morn.
DU MAURIER. *Trilby.*

APRIL 11

WE are apt to be kinder to the brutes that
love us than to the women that love
us. Is it because the brutes are dumb?
GEORGE ELIOT. *Adam Bede.*

APRIL 12

A LOVING creature she, and brave,
And fondly tries her struggling friend to save.
WORDSWORTH. *A Dog's Tragedy.*

APRIL 13

HIS good hound for weal or woe,
Would not from his master go,
Buy lay licking his woundes.
He meanys to have helped him again,
Thereto he did all his main;
Great kindness is in houndis.
Mediaeval Metrical Romance.

APRIL 14

NOT for myself. . . . I assure you. Like Atè's
golden apple, it shall go to the fairest.
. . . Here, Bran!
KINGSLEY. *Hypatia.*

APRIL 15

WELL of all dogs it stands confessed
Your English bulldogs are the best.
I say it, and will set my hand to 't,
Camden records it, and I'll stand to 't.
SMART. *Insular Prejudice.*

APRIL 16

NATURE never makes a ferret in the shape of
a mastiff.
GEORGE ELIOT.

APRIL 17

MUST I feel an equal warmth towards my
bosom friend and his greyhound?
T. HOOD.

APRIL 18

THE fleetest, bravest hound
That ever coursed on hill or lea,
Or swept the heathy ground.
MARY RUSSELL MITFORD.

APRIL 19

A FRANKLYN'S dogge leped over a style,
And hys name was littel Byngo.
Ingoldsby Legends. Lay of S. Glenulphus.

APRIL 20

SO, when two dogs are fighting in the streets,
With a third dog, one of the two dogs meets,
With angry teeth he beats him to the bone,
And this dog smarts for what that dog has done.
FIELDING. *Tom Thumb the Great.*

KING GEORGE III.
With his Beagles at Windsor

APRIL 21

WELL, dogs cannot lie, or bribe, or pick a lock,
Or go bull-baiting in share markets, or pre-side
As chairmen over public companies!
OUIDA. *Puck.*

APRIL 22

HERE lies poor Nick, an honest creature,
Of faithful, gently, courteous nature.
SYDNEY SMITH.

APRIL 23

CALM, though not mean, courageous without rage,
Serious not dull, and without thinking, sage:
Pleased at the lot that nature has assigned,
Snarl as I list, and freely bark my mind.
W. HAMILTON. *The Dog Incog.*

APRIL 24

HE has known me in all that has happened;
haven't you, Jip? And I couldn't bear to
slight him because he was a little altered.
DICKENS. *David Copperfield.*

APRIL 25

I DO allow him to be as familiar with me as
my dog.
SHAKESPEARE. *Henry IV., ii. 2.*

APRIL 26

I ROSE with the dawn: with my dog as my
guide.
BYRON. *Young Highlander.*

APRIL 27

BUT Maddalo was travelling far away,
Among the mountains of Armenia.
His dog was dead.
SHELLEY. *Julian and Maddalo.*

APRIL 28

OTHER dogs in thymey dew
Tracked the hares and followed through
Sunny moor and meadow. . . .
E. B. BROWNING. *To my Dog.*

APRIL 29

ALL the hedges are white with dust, and the
great dog under the creaking wain
Hangs his head in the lazy heat, while onward
the horses toil and strain.
LONGFELLOW. *The Golden Legend.*

APRIL 30

GIVE a child while he craves, and a dog while
his tail doth wag, and you shall have a
fair dog and a foul knave.
Old Proverb.

NOTES

SCENES AT THE WINDHOLME KENNELS, ISLIP, LONG ISLAND

MAY

A sensible dog takes human beings as he finds them. They have their good points and their bad points (some have no points at all), but they mean well, and they are the most intelligent animals we have.

STEPHEN TOWNSEND.
A Thoroughbred Mongrel.

MAY 01

AND close beside him, in the snow,
Poor Yarrow, partner of their woe,
Crouches upon his master's breast
And licks his cheek to break his rest.
SCOTT. *Marmion.*

MAY 02

AS true a dog as ever fought at head.
SHAKESPEARE. *King Lear, iv. 6.*

He'd been a good 'un in his time.
HORSFIELD.

MAY 03

I OFFERED her my own, who is a dog as big as ten of yours, and therefore a gift the greater.
SHAKESPEARE. *Two Gentlemen of Verona, iv. 4.*

MAY 04

WE canna meet Him no fairer, no better, than wi' hands as niver hae harmed the poor dumb beast.
OUIDA. *Puck.*

MAY 05

HE was a joy. It was good to go to sleep
and know he would be there in the
morning.
DU MAURIER. *Trilby.*

MAY 06

THE deep-mouthed bark
Comes nigher still and nigher;
Bursts on the path a dark bloodhound,
His tawny muzzle tracked the ground,
And his red eye shot fire.
SCOTT. *Lay of the Last Minstrel.*

MAY 07

OH! Where does faithful Gelert roam,
The flower of his race?
So true, so brave; a lamb at home,
A lion in the chase!
SPENSER. *Gelert*

MAY 08

A LOVING creature, she, and brave.
WORDSWORTH. *Incident.*

DOGS bark as they are bred. . . .
Old Proverb.

ALDERSHOT BEAGLES.
The Pack and Field at Farley Castle.

MAY 09

QUIEN a su péno quiere matar,
Eabia le ha levantar.
Spanish Proverb.

MAY 10

NO serious order did he e'er forget,
      No loving friend;
He was as true a heart as could be met
      To the world's end.
HORNE. *Beth Gellert.*

MAY 11

AND yet thou should'st have lived!
SOUTHEY. *On the Death of a Favourite Dog.*

LOVE me, love my dog. . . .
Proverb.

MAY 12

WHEN I feel happy my tail almost wags me
off my legs, but when I pretend to be
happy, it flops about with as much spirit
as a wet rag on a still day.
STEPHEN TOWNSEND.

MAY 13

FIERCE, bounding sprang the ship,
Like greyhound starting from the slip
To seize his flying prey.
SCOTT. *Lord of the Isles.*

MAY 14

AND in that town a dog was found,
As many dogs there be;
Both mongrel, puppy, whelp, and hound,
And curs of low degree.
GOLDSMITH. *Mad Dog.*

MAY 15

IF Gyp had had a tail he would doubtless have
wagged it, but being destitute of that
vehicle for his emotions, he was, like many
other worthy persons, destined to appear
more phlegmatic than nature had made him.
GEORGE ELIOT. *Adam Bede.*

MAY 16

THIS dog only . . . crept and crept
Next a languid cheek that slept,
Sharing in the shadow.
E. B. BROWNING. *To Flush.*

MAY 17

MEN who loved dogs were always pitiful.
OUIDA.

I SHALL make Jip race, he is getting quite
old and lazy.
DICKENS. *David Copperfield.*

MAY 18

SHE could turn a knight into a wagon of hay,
Or two nice little boys into puppies at play.
Ingoldsby Legends. Bleeding Heart Yard.

MAY 19

AS a dog keeps his master's root,
Bidding the plunderer stand aloof.
SCOTT. *Rokeby.*

MAY 20

HE wasn't a bit intellectual, and thought more
of chasing a sheep on the hillside than of
psychological discussion.
TOWNSEND. *A Thoroughbred Mongrel.*

From a Coloured Print in Cynographia Britannica (Sydenham Edwards) published in 1803.

MAY 21

THE deep-mouthed bloodhound's heavy bay
Resounded up the rocky way.
SCOTT. *Lady of the Lake.*

MAY 22

TWO curs shall tame each other: pride alone
Must tarre the mastiffs on, as 'twere their bone.
SHAKESPEARE. *Troilus and Cressida, i. 3.*

MAY 23

A PARLOUR pet unspoiled by favour,
A pattern of good dog behaviour.
SYDNEY SMITH.

MAY 24

MY love shall hear the music of my hounds
Uncouple in the western valley; let them go.
SHAKESPEARE. *Midsummer Night's Dream, iv. I.*

MAY 25

HE that strikes my dog would strike me, if he durst.
Old Proverb.

MAY 26

LOOK! A horse at the door,
    And little King Charley snarling!
Go back, my lord, across the moor,
    You are not her darling.
TENNYSON. *Maud, xii. 8.*

MAY 27

IN a corner of the buzzing shade
The house-dog, with the vacant greyhound, lies
Outstretched and sleepy.
THOMSON. *Seasons.*

MAY 28

NATURE teaches beasts to know their friends.
SHAKESPEARE. *Coriolanus, ii. I.*

DOGS that bark at a distance never bite.
Old Proverb.

MAY 29

IF you will couple up an ordinary low-country greyhound with a Highland wolf-dog, you must not blame the first of them for taking the direction it pleases the last to drag him in.
SCOTT. *Fair Maid of Perth.*

MAY 30

TWO dogs strive for a bone and the third runs away with it.
Proverb.

MAY 31

THEY called us – for our fierceness – English dogs!
SHAKESPEARE. *Henry VI., i. 5.*

GIVE a dog a bad name and you may as well hang him.
Proverb.

ALDERSHOT BEAGLES.
The Pack and Field at Farley Castle.

JUNE

They were friends in a friendship closer than brotherhood. . . . His heart awakened to a mighty love, which never wavered once in its fidelity while life abode with him. . . . And being a dog he was grateful.

OUIDA. Dog of Flanders.

JUNE 01

WHEN mastiffs fight, little dogs bark.
Old Proverb.

THE fleetest hound in all the North.
SCOTT. *Lady of the Lake.*

JUNE 02

TO assume a semblance the very dogs disclaimed.
SHAKESPEARE. *King Lear, iv. 6.*

JUNE 03

ON the drawbridge the warder stout,
Saw a terrier and lurcher passing out.
SCOTT. *Lay of the Last Minstrel.*

JUNE 04

THE shepherd doth not kill the sheep that
wander from his flock, but send
His careful dog to bring them to the fold.
TENNYSON. *Queen Mary, iii. 4.*

JUNE 05

SOUVENT à mauvais chien tombe un bon os
en gueule.
French Proverb.

JUNE 06

WHEN every terrier rough and grim,
And greyhound with his length of limb;
And pointer, now employ'd no more,
Cumber our parlour's narrow floor.
SCOTT. *Marmion.*

JUNE 07

IF the dog bark, go in;
If the bitch bark, go out.
Hebrew Proberb.

JUNE 08

THE first I'll name, they ca'd him Caesar,
Was keepit for his Honour's pleasure;
His hair, his size, his mouth, his lugs,
Show'd he was nane o' Scotland's dogs.
BURNS. *The Twa Dogs.*

GROUP OF MR. A GORHAM'S ROUGH-COATED BEAGLES.
Photograph by Russell and Sons.

JUNE 09

BETTER to be a liar's dog, and hold my master honest.
TENNYSON. *Harold III., I.*

JUNE 10

HIS good hound, for weal or woe,
Would not from his master go.
UNKNOWN. *Mediaeval Romance.*

JUNE 11

MY spaniel, prettiest of his race,
And high in pedigree.
COWPER. *Dog and Water-Lily.*

JUNE 12

SIR WALTER, restless as the veering wind,
Calls to the few tired dogs that yet remain.
WORDSWORTH. *Hart-Leap Well.*

JUNE 13

FORESTERS in green-wood trim
Lead in the leash the gazehounds grim
SCOTT. *Marmion.*

JUNE 14

THEN from the plaintive mother's teat he took
Her blind and shuddering puppies, naming each,
And naming those, his friends, for whom they were.
TENNYSON. *The Brook.*

JUNE 15

THE best dog leaps the stile first.

DOGS that put up many hares, eat none.
Old Proverbs.

JUNE 16

THOU didst love to lick the hand that fed thee;
Even life itself was comfort.
SOUTHEY. *On the Death of a Dog.*

JUNE 17

HE looked the oddest, wee-set, waywardest,
most whimsical little doglet in the world.
TOWNSEND. *Thoroughbred Mongrel.*

JUNE 18

THERE was Yap, the queer white and brown
terrier, with one ear turned back, trotting
about and sniffing vaguely, as though he
were in search of a companion.
GEORGE ELIOT. *Mill on the Floss.*

JUNE 19

GET thee hence and find my dog again.
SHAKESPEARE. *Two Gentlemen of Verona, iv. 4.*

JUNE 20

HE could carry, and fetch, and run after a stick,
Could well understand, the word of command.
Ingoldsby Legends. Bagman's Dog.

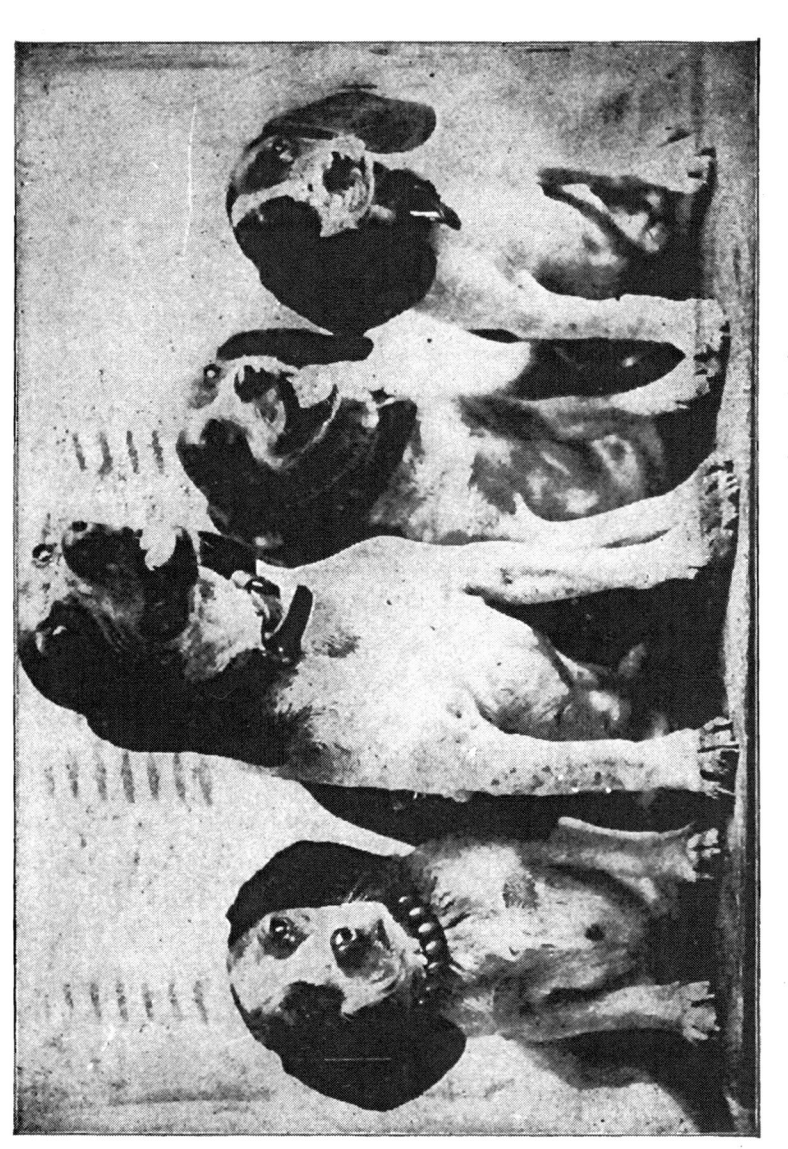

"As Pretty as a Picture." (Beagles.)

JUNE 21

"WE hounds killed the hare," quoth the lapdog.
Old Proverb.

JUNE 22

LET a be the hound, man, let a be the hound;
Kilbuck mauna be guided that gate
neither.
SCOTT. *Black Dwarf.*

JUNE 23

CAÓ que muito ladra nunca bom pera caça.
Portuguese Proverb.

JUNE 24

I CARRIED Mistress Silvia the dog you bade me.
SHAKESPEARE. *Two Gentlemen of Verona, iv. 4.*

JUNE 25

EVERY dog is eager hearted.
WORDSWORTH. *Incident.*

JUNE 26

MY dog, now lost in flags and reeds,
    Now starting into sight;
Pursued the swallow on the mead
    With scarce a slower flight.
COWPER. *Beau and the Water-Lily.*

JUNE 27

FORTUNATELY we dogs have powers of telepathy unknown to humans.
TOWNSEND. *Thoroughbred Mongrel.*

JUNE 28

HIS valour and his vigilance
Became a proverb of the vale;
His instincts made a small romance,
And shepherd boys preserved each tale.
HORNE.

JUNE 29

THE slowhound wakes the fox's lair,
The greyhound presses on the hare.
SCOTT. *Rokeby*.

JUNE 30

HE'S gone to seek his dog; which, by his
master's commands, he must carry for a
present to his lady.
SHAKESPEARE. *Two Gentlemen of Verona, iv. 2.*

NOTES

BEAGLE

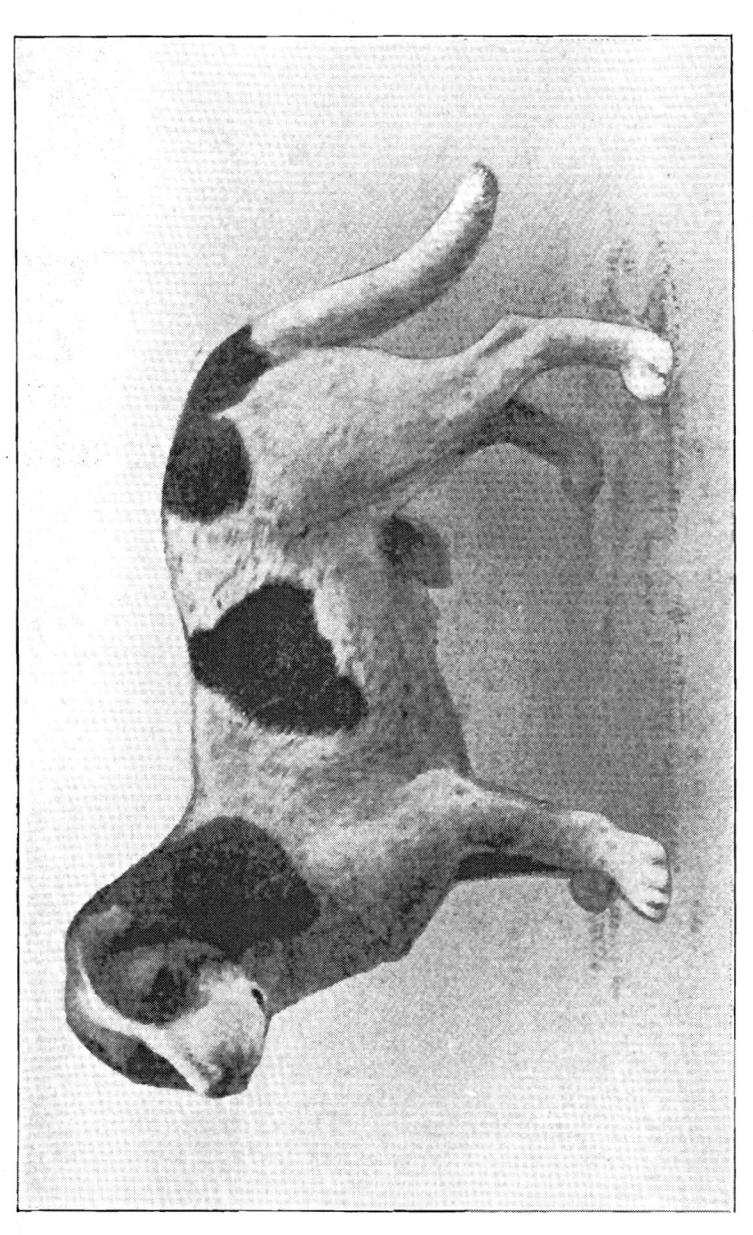

To face page 182

HOUNDS

JULY

It is easy enough to cock one's ears and to caper about with a fictitious gaiety, but the tail has a personality of its own, and always gives us dogs away….if only I had my tail under control, I should be the most successful and charming liar in the world.

                    TOWNSEND.
                     A Thoroughbred Mongrel.

JULY 01

THE almighty, who gave the dog to be the
companion of our pleasures and out toils,
hath invested him with a nature noble
and incapable of deceit.
SIR WALTER SCOTT.

JULY 02

SO they went fourth both, and the young man's
dog with them.
Tobit, v. 16

JULY 03

WITH eye upraised, his master's look to scan,
The joy, the solace, and the aid of man.
CRABBE.

JULY 04

HE followit him where'er he gaed,
Sae that the hound him lovit sae,
That he wald part nae wise him frae.
BARBOUR. *Bruce and the blood hound*

JULY 05

A dog howls loud and long,
And now, as guided by the voice of Heaven,
Digs with his feet, …
A man lies underneath! Let us to work.
ROGERS. *Barry the St. Bernard.*

JULY 06

…EVEN to the beast
That lacks discourse of reason, but too oft
With uncorrupted feeling and dumb faith
Puts lordly man to shame.
SOUTHEY. *Roderick's Faithful Theron.*

JULY 07

SO all forsook him, all save one –
One humble, faithful, powerless slave-
His dog, old Nina.
CAROLINE SOUTHEY. *The Tale of Reign of Terrier.*

JULY 08

NEVER was a puppy so *bien instruit,*
Or possessed of such natural talent, as he.
BARHAM. *Bagman's Dog.*

Photo] [*Fall*

BEAGLE : *Melody of Reynalton*, the property of Mrs. Elms of 433 Brixton Road, S.W. 9.

JULY 09

THE rich man's guardian, and the poor man's friend;
The only creature faithful to the end.
CRABBE.

JULY 10

THOUGH the mastiff be gentle, yet bite him not on the lip.
Old proverb

JULY 11

HIS faithful dog, rough Gelert, wit them sped,
…He was as true as heart as could be met
To the world's end.
HORNE. *Beth Gelert.*

JULY 12

ALL human ties alas! Are ropes of sand,
… But never yet the dog our bounty fed,
Betrayed the kindness, or forgot the bread.
LYTTON. *Gwaine and the Hound.*

JULY 13

BY the angel Raphael guided,
Went the faithful dog, and good.
MARY HOWITT. *Tobias' Dog*

JULY 14

FAÄITHFUL an' True- them words be i' Scriptur
-an' Faäithful an' True
'Ull be fun' upo' four short legs ten times fur
one an' upo' two.
TENNYSON. *Owd Roä*

JULY 15

SIGN me a hero!...
Over the balustrade has bounced
A mere, instinctive dog…
How well he dives!
R.BONING. *Tray: A Hero*

JULY 16

THE knight had another jewel
That he loved so well:
A greyhound that was good and snel,
And the knight loved it well.
UNKNOWN. *Medieval Romance.*

JULY 17

OH, Indra, and what of this dog? It hath
faithfully followed me through:
Let it go with me into heaven, for my soul
is full of compassion.
Indian Hero's Creed.

JULY 18

MY hounds are bred out of the Spartan kind,
So flewed, so sanded;...
Matched in mouth like bells-
A cry more tuneable was never hollaed to.
SHAKESPEARE . *Sonnet*

JULY 19

NOR last, forget my faithful dogs.
DRYDEN
'TIS an ill dog that deserves not a crust.
Old proverb.

JULY 20

I WAS a dog much in respect for doughty deed.
HAMILTON. *Bonny Heck.*

THE BEST BEAGLE TYPE.

Here is a true champion of his breed—"Dauntless of Reynalton"—owned by Mrs. N. E. Elms. Time and again in many parts he has carried all before him. He won the 1934 Challenge Certificate at Cruft's. This view shows all his excellent body points and for a closer appreciation of his magnificent head the reader is referred to page 167.

JULY 21

A ROLICKSOME, frolicsome, rare old cock
As ever did nothing was our dog Jock;
A gleesome, fleasome, affectionate beast,
As slow at a fight, as swift at a feast.
PAYN. *Our Dog Jock.*

JULY 22

YOU are not so old, Jiip, are you, that you'll leave your mother yet? We may keep each other a little longer.
DICKENS. *David Copperfield.*

JULY 23

TRUSTED and faithful, tried and true,
Watchful and swift to do my will;
Grateful for care that was thy due,
To duty's call obedient still.
FANNY KEMBLE. *On an Irish Terrier.*

JULY 24

KIND and courteous, and faithful and true,
Qualities, Tray, that were found in you.
BARHAM. *The Cynotaph.*

JULY 25

PRAY steal me not; I'm Mrs. Dingley's,
Whose heart in this four footed thing lies.
SWIFT. *On The Collar of a Tiger.*

JULY 26

MY Bawty is a cur I dearly like.
RAMSEY

BRAG is a good dog but Holdfast is better.
Old Proverb.

JULY 27

MY dog, the trustiest of his kind,
With gratitude inflames my mind;
I mark his true, his faithful way,
And in my service copy Tray.
GAY. *Tray, the Exemplar.*

JULY 28

MY master wants no key of state,
For Bounce can keep his house and gate.
UNKNOWN

JULY 29

I HAVE known many so-called Christians who have neither the amiability nor the discrimination of this dog.
GEORGE LEWES.

JULY 30

TRUELOVE, his hound so good,
Helped his master, and by him stood.
Mediaval Romance.

JULY 31

WHEN fatigued, on the grass the shepherd would lie…
His faithful companion crawled constantly nigh.
PETER PINDAR. *Old Friends.*

A MOMENT'S RESPITE.

Hounds when hunting are very thirsty, more especially in the early days of the season. They seldom stop to drink, however, when on the scent, but occasionally will take time thirst during a lull in the proceedings.

AUGUST

Dogs are judges of character, and are seldom mistaken in their intuitive likes and dislikes. There is no animal possessing one tithe of the qualifications of the dog for the various purposes by which he is used by man — a woman's pet, a man's companion, a vigilant sentry, a powerful and valiant ally, and the most faithful and truest of friends.

HENTY.

AUGUST 01

THIS dog only, watched in reach
Of a faintly-uttered speech
Or a louder sighing.
E.B. Browning. *To Flush.*

AUGUST 02

AND now I'm in the world alone-
But why should I for others groan
When none will sigh for me?
Perhaps my dog will whine in vain.
BYRON. *Childe Harold.*

AUGUST 03

HE has the staunch Cyme-hound to track the
wounded buck hill and dale; but he
hath also the fleet gazehound to kill him
at view.
SIR W SCOTT. *Kenilworth.*

AUGUST 04

THEY were coming, dowered with blessings,
And the dog with joyous barking
Told the same, as best he could.
MARY HOWITT. *Tobias' Dog*

AUGUST 05

BUT I meäns fur to maäke 'is owd aäge as
'appy as iver I can,
Fur I owäs owd roäver moor nor I iver owäd
mottal man.
TENNYSON. *Owd Roä*

AUGUST 06

A BULLDOG of the true British breed
SIR W. SCOTT. *The Pirate*

Have a care of a silent dog.
Old Proverb

AUGUST 07

A BARK, loud, open, and free,
As an honest old watch-dog's bark should be.
Ingoldsby Legends. The Witches' Frolic.

AUGUST 08

ANIMALS are such agreeable friends; they ask
no questions, they pass no criticisms.
GEORGE ELIOT.

By courtesy of] [*Dr. Jobson-Scott.*
A CHECK.
Apparently the hare has passed through a wood and the scent has been lost, the Beagles not knowing which way to go. A Hound on the left side of the picture thinks he has found the scent.

AUGUST 09

DEAR little friend, who, day by day,
Before the door of home,
Art ready waiting till thy master come,
With monitory paw and noise.
LEWIS MORRIS.

AUGUST 10

OF all the boons that men possess,
To aid to cheer, instruct and bless;
The dog ... bold, fond and beauteous beast,
Is far from either last, or least.
ELIZA COOK.

AUGUST 11

MEGLIO é esser capo di lucertola
Che coda di dragone.
Italian Proverb

AUGUST 12

HE is the dog of one now dead; ...
His strength, his plight, his speed so light,
You had with wonder viewed.
MAGINN. *Odysseus and Argus.*

AUGUST 13

SURMOUNTING e'en her timid nature,
Love brought her to the prison door,
And there she crouched fond and faithful creature!
CAROLINE SOUTHEY. *Tale of the Reign of Terrier.*

AUGUST 14

A HEALTH to the noble, the honest old Tray,
The watchman of night, the companion of day.
ELIZA COOK.

AUGUST 15

ONE hound he had, both curious and bold,
Pleasant, but peir and full of pulchritude,
Supple and swift, and in all game richt gude.
STEWART. *Battle about a Dog.*

AUGUST 16

AN old dog cannot alter his way of barking.
Old Proverb.

BLESSINGS on thee, dog of mine.
E.B BROWNING.

AUGUST 17

"NO," said he, "I will now take a bribe to betray my master."
Aesop's Fables.

AUGUST 18

HE must have a piece of flannel in his basket this winter, and I shouldn't wonder if he came out quite fresh again with the flowers in the spring.
DICKENS. *David Copperfield.*

AUGUST 19

WHEN up they gat, and shook their lugs,
Rejoiced they were na men, but dogs!
BURNS. *Twa Dogs.*

AUGUST 20

AND a song for the dog shall be merrily trolled,
As the meed of the faithful, the fond and the bold.
ELIZA COOK.

BEAGLE PUPPIES.
A jolly group of youngsters a few weeks old.

AUGUST 21

HE listens for his trusty hounds.
SCOTT. *The Wild Huntsman.*

THE best dog leaps the stile first
Old Proverb.

AUGUST 22

ALL other houndis he did exceed sae far
As into licht the moon does near ilk star.
STEWART. *Battle about a Dog.*

AUGUST 23

LOVED Towser was his heart's delight,
Entrusted with the flocks at night,
And guardian in the field.
GALDEN. *Towser.*

AUGUST 24

OLD dogs bark not for nothing.
Proverb.

THE hounds ... divide, the loved caresses
of the mind.
SCOTT. *The Island.*

AUGUST 25

OLD dogs bark not for nothing.
Proverb.

THE hounds ... divide, the loved caresses
of the mind.
SCOTT. *The Island.*

AUGUST 26

THEY watched a cur before the miser's gate-
Gaunt, savage, shaggy, with an eye that shone...
His master prized him much.
CRABBE. *The Miser's only Friend.*

AUGUST 27

TO abandon the faithful and devoted is an endless
crime, like the murder of a Brahmin;
Never, therefore, come weal or woe, will I abandon
yon faithful dog.
Indian Hero's Creed.

AUGUST 28

TWO dogs of black St. Hubert's breed,
Unmatched for courage, breath, and speed,
Fast on his flying traces came.
SCOTT. *The Chase*

AUGUST 29

WHEN a dog has any trouble with a well-bred biped, one may bet one's last biscuit it is generally his own fault.
TOWNSEND. *Thoroughbred Mongrel.*

AUGUST 30

QUI veut battre son chien trouve assez de batons.
French Proverb.

I WATCH the dog, I watch the gate.
MASSEY.

AUGUST 31

FROM many a day-dream has thy short, quick bark
Recalled my soul.
SOUTHEY. *Death of a Favourite Dog.*

Photo] [*Sport & General*
A CHAMPION BEAGLE BITCH.
"Bangle", shown here, was exhibited at the Peterborough Hound Show She was one of the Ampleforth College pack, of Ampleforth Yorkshire.

SEPTEMBER

Then here we halt on the horns of a dilemma. Everyone with large acquaintance, with decent and "gentle-man like" dogs, must admit their share in the highest humanities;... yet shall we, because we walk on our hind feet, assume to ourselves only the privilege of imperishability? Shall we, who are even as they, though we wag our tongues and not out tails, demand a special providence and a selfish salvation?

GEORGE ELIOT.

SEPTEMBER 01

POOR Tray Charmant!
Poor Tray de mon ami!
Dogberry and Verges.

HUMBLE his mind, tho' great his wit.
SOMERVILLE. *All Accomplished Rover.*

SEPTEMBER 02

WITH eye of sloe. With ear not low,
With horse's breast with depth of chest,
With breadth of loin, and curve in groin,
With nape far set behind the head:
Such were the dogs that Fingal bred.
Old Celtic Poem.

SEPTEMBER 03

ALTHOUGH I mean not to disparage the deedes
of Alexander's horse, I will match my
dogge against him for good carriage.
SIR JOHN DAVIES in 1608.

SEPTEMBER 04

ROUND this sepulchral spot,
Emblems of hope we twine;
If God be Love, what sleeps below was not
Without a spark divine.
Miss W. Wynn on the Death of her Dog.

SEPTEMBER 05

OUR doggie he cam' home at e'en
And scarted both his lugs, O!
Quo he, "If folks had only tails,
They'd be maist as gude as dogs, O!
MACLEOD. *The Waggin' o' our Dog's Tail.*

SEPTEMBER 06

THEREFORE to this dog will I,
Tenderly, not scornfully,
Render praise and favour.
E. B BROWNING. *To Flush, my Dog.*

SEPTEMBER 07

OH! What shall I do for a dog?
HOOD. *Lament of the Blind.*

MY faithful, grateful Hector!
HOGG. *My Auld Hector.*

SEPTEMBER 08

I WATCH the door, I watch the gate,
I'm watching early, watching late-
Your doggie still- I watch and wait!
MASSEY. *Dead Boy's Dog.*

A MUDDLED SCENT

The Worcester Park and Buckland Beagles at Rowgardens Park. Charlwood, are having difficulty in finding the scent. This may possibly be due to the presence of cattle in the background.

(Sport & General)

IN FULL CRY.

The Master of the West Surrey and Horsell Park keeps up with the pack, watching its behaviour intently. The actions of the dogs provide him with useful information.

SEPTEMBER 09

AND so my dog and I have met, and sworn
Fresh love and fealty for another morn.
RAWNSLEY. *My dog and I.*

SEPTEMBER 10

DO the work that's nearest,
Tho' it's dull at whiles;
Helping, when you meet them,
Lame dogs over stiles.
C.KINGSLEY

SEPTEMBER 11

HIS lungs are good enough, and his dislikes
are not at all feeble. He has a good
many years before him, no doubt.
DICKENS. *David Copperfield.*

SEPTEMBER 12

HE would wag his three miles of a tail, and
utter soft whimperings of welcome in his
dreams.
DU MAURIER. *Trilby.*

SEPTEMBER 13

SEE how yon terrier gently leads along
The feeble beggar to his 'customed stand.
PRATT. *Blind Man's Dog.*

SEPTEMBER 14

THE dog and I are both grown old…
I marked his look of faithful care,
I placed my hand on his shaggy side-
"There is a sun that shines above,
A sun that shines on both," I cried.
BOWLES. *Grown Old Together.*

SEPTEMBER 15

MY Dog! What remedy remains,
Since, teach you all I can;
I see you, after all my pains,
So much resemble man.
COWPER. *Beau and the Bird.*

SEPTEMBER 16

THUS is there a moral obligation between a man and a dog.
WOLCOT.

SEPTEMBER 17

"WHAT is become of your dog, Sir John?"
"Gone to heaven," was the answer.
SOUTHEY. *Common Place Book.*

SEPTEMBER 18

AND the dog is still the faithful,
Still the loving friend of man;
Ever ready at his bidding,
Doing for him all he can.
Sketches of Natural History.

SEPTEMBER 19

THE drawing-room was made for dogs,
Not dogs for the drawing room.
RHODA BROUGHTON. *The Game and the Candle.*

SEPTEMBER 20

GIVE I back more love again
Than dogs often take of men,
Learning from my human.
E.B.BROWNING. *To Flush, my Dog.*

[*Photo.*] ARRIVING AT THE MEET. [*Sport & General.*]

In the olden days packs travelled to the nearest meets on their own feet or in a farm cart, but to-day they are transported by a motor van specially built for this purpose, allowing adequate ventilation; notice front of van and affording the men in charge facilities to keep an eye on them. Care is taken to steady the Hounds as they jump down. Those shown are the West Surrey and Horsell Park Beagles.

SEPTEMBER 21

WHATEVER sad mischance o'ertake ye,
Man, here is ane will hald ye dear!
Man, here is ane will ne'er forsake ye!
HOGG. *My Auld Hector.*

SEPTEMBER 22

ISSA, than a maid more fond;
Issa, Indian gems beyond;
Issa, most enchanting chub!
Pup, the darling of my Pub!
ELPHINSTON. *Issa's Portrait.*

SEPTEMBER 23

TRUE from the first, and faithful to the end,
I balk no mistress, and forsake no friend,...
A very plain and downright honest dog.
WILLIAM HAMILTON. *The Dog Incog.*

SEPTEMBER 24

LO, the poor Indian! Whose untutor'd mind
Sees God in clouds, or hears Him in the wind;
... Thinks, admitted to that equal sky,
His faithful dog shall bear him company.
POPE. *A Simple Faith.*

SEPTEMBER 25

THOU art as fair and comely as a dog,
Thou art as true and honest as a dog,
Thou art as kind and liberal as a dog,
Thou art as wise and valiant as a dog!
DAVIES. *In Cineam.*

SEPTEMBER 26

AND now at last (good faith) I plainly see,
That dogs, more wise than women, friendly be.
TUBERVILLE. *Love Me, Love my Dog.*

SEPTEMBER 27

OF any beast none is more faithful found,…
Nor keeps his master's person or his goods
With greater care than doth the dog or hound.
MOLLE. *The Faithfullest Beast.*

SEPTEMBER 28

I NEVER barked when out of season,
I never bit without reason;
I ne'er insulted weaker brother,
Nor wronged by force or fraud another.
BLACKLOCK. *A Proud Boast.*

SEPTEMBER 29

OF all the dogges near your father's courte,
not one hathe more love, more diligence
to please, or less paye for pleasinge, than
him I write of.
Sir J Davies to Prince Henry, 1608

SEPTEMBER 30

BRUTE, with a heart of human love
And speechless soul of instinct fine!
How few by reason's law who more
Deserve an epitaph like thine.
FANNY KEMBLE. *On an Irish Retriever.*

NOTES

A FAMOUS PAINTING OF BEAGLES.
Maud Earl painted Miss Oughton's pack of Beagles about 1899, showing the pack discovering the hare when least expecting to find it.

OCTOBER

And this dog was satisfied
If a pale, thin hand would glide
Down his dewlaps sloping-
Which he pushed his nose within
After platforming his chin
On the palm left open…
Yet blessed to the height
Of all good, and all delight,
Previous to thy nature-
Only loved beyond that line
With a love that answers time,
Loving fellow creature.

E.B.BROWNING.
To Flush, my Dog.

OCTOBER 01

BUT chief myself I will enjoin,
Awake at Duty's call;
To show a love as prompt as thine,
To him who gives me all.
COWPER. *Beau and the Water Lily.*

OCTOBER 02

FOR herself she hath no fears,
Him alone she sees and hears.
WORDSWORTH. *Incident.*

OCTOBER 03

AS for brute animals, and things undignified
with reason, use them generously and
nobly.
MARCUS AURELIUS.

OCTOBER 04

WHAT are ye all, dear creatures tame and wild,
What other nature yours, than of a child!
LEWIS MORRIS. *To the Tormentors.*

OCTOBER 05

WE hae a dog that wags his tail
(He's abit of a wag himsel', O!)
Every day he gangs down the town,
At nicht he's news to tell, O!
MACLEOD. *The Waggin' o' our Dog's Tail.*

OCTOBER 06

MY dog loves me, but could he look beyond
His earthly master, would his love extend
To Him… I will not doubt.
HOLMES. *Questions.*

OCTOBER 07

UNDERNEATH my stroking hand,
Startled eyes of hazel bland,
Kindling, growing larger.
E.B BROWNING. *To Flush, my Dog.*

OCTOBER 08

DON and Sancho, Tranp and Tray,
On the parlour steps collected;
Wagged their tails, and seemed to say:
"Our master knows you, you're expected!"
PRAED. *Dog's Welcome.*

THE BEAGLE HEAD.

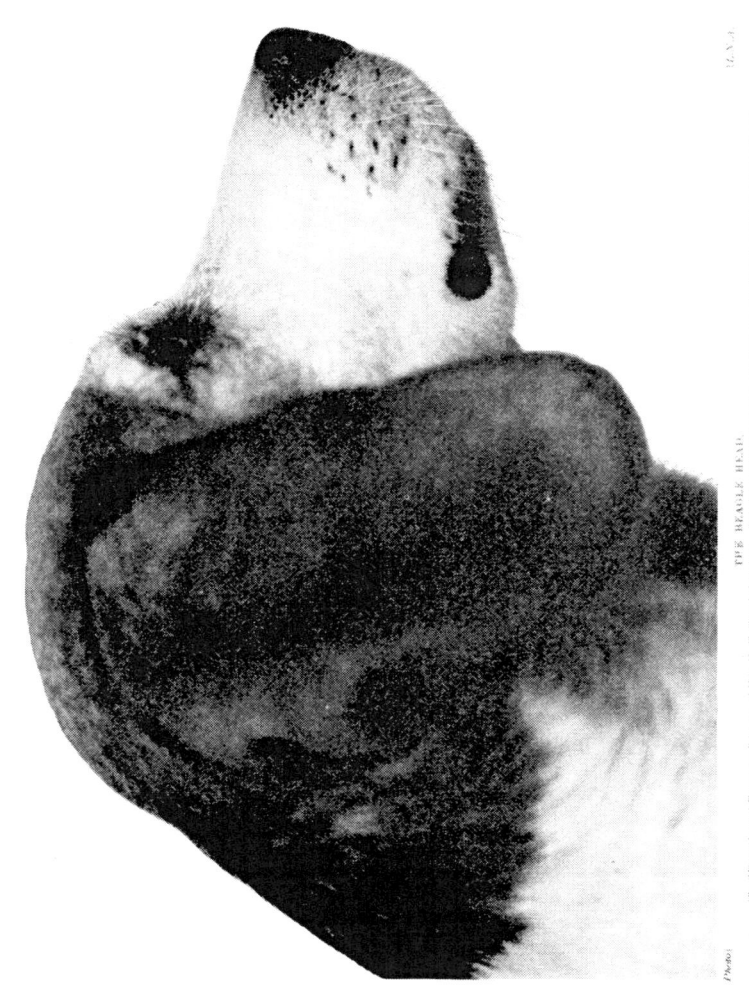

Ch. "Dauntless of Reynalton" is one of Mrs. N. E. Elms's breeding. It is interesting to compare the head with that of Ch. "Fairground" on page 96. It is a fine example of what the head of a modern Beagle should be.

OCTOBER 09

THE sleek and the gamesome, the swift and the bold,
At surprise, I wakened to hear thy proud bark,
With the coo of the house dove, the lay of the lark.
MOIR. *Dying Oscar.*

OCTOBER 10

AY, his friend; for where shall there ever be found
A friend like his resolute, fond, bloodhound.
BARRY CORNWALL. *My Bloodhound.*

OCTOBER 11

'TIS sweet to know there is an eye will mark
Our coming, and look brighter when we come.
BRYON. *The Watch Dog.*

OCTOBER 12

MY poor old Chloe! Gentle playfellow,
Most patient, most enduring was thy love.
CAROLINE SOUTHEY. *On Trust.*

OCTOBER 13

MY playful cat, and honest dog,
Are all the friends I have.
ELIOT. *My Only Friends.*

OCTOBER 14

SAY thou wilt course; thy greyhounds are as
swift
As breathéd stags, aye, fleeter than the roe.
SHAKESPEARE.
Taming of the Shrew. Induction, Scene 2.

OCTOBER 15

NOW let Ulysses praise his dogge Argus…
Yet could I say such things of my Bungey
as might shame them both, either for
good faith, clear wit, or wonderful deedes.
SIR JOHN DAVIES.

OCTOBER 16

COME, my auld towzy, trusty friend…
All wordly cares we'll leave behind.
HOGG. *To Hector.*

OCTOBER 17

DOG Rover shall confute you all;…
Can apprehend, judge, syllogise…
Is often wiser than his master.
SOMERVILLE. *All-Accomplished Rover.*

OCTOBER 18

BEHOLD this creature's form and state
Which Nature therefore did create,
That to the world might be expressed
What mien there can be in a beast.
K. PHILLIPS. *The Greyhound.*

OCTOBER 19

ARE clepped all by the name of dogs; the valued file
Distinguished the swift, the slow, the subtle,
The housekeeper, the hunter, everyone according
To the gift which bounteous nature hath in him closed.
SHAKESPEARE. *Macbeth, iii. I*

OCTOBER 20

HE called his dog (that sometime had the praise)
Whitefoot, well known to all that kept the plain.
DRAYTON. *Farewell to Whitefoot.*

ON PARADE.

Like father, like son—a youngster takes stock of some of the best of the South Herts Beagles at the Kennels at Baldock. The reader should notice how much better are the ears of these Beagles than of some of the exhibition type.

OCTOBER 21

PUT on thy envious spectacles, and see...
The dog is gracèd, comparèd with great Banks,
Both beasts right famous for their pretty pranks.
HARINGTON.

OCTOBER 22

CALL him, he leaves his game and comes to thee
With wagging tail, off'ring his service meek.
MOLLE. *The Faithfullest Beast.*

OCTOBER 23

NOR words nor honours can enough commend
The social dog-nay , more- the faithful friend.
UNKNOWN.

OCTOBER 24

IS a man a hopeless heathen if he dreams of one fair day,
When, with spirit free from shadows grey and cold,
He may wander thro' the heather in the "unknown far away"
With his good old dog before him, as of old?
HORSFIELD. *Old Rocket.*

OCTOBER 25

BUT all those virtues which commend...
Were thine in store, thou faithful friend,
A mate how dear!
MATTHEW ARNOLD. *Kasier Dead.*

OCTOBER 26

FOR thou didst give to me, old friend,
Thy service while thy life did last.
FANNY KEMBLE. *On an Irish Retriever.*

OCTOBER 27

THE fleetest, bravest hound
That ever coursed on hill or lea
... My Marmion!
MARY R. MITFORD. *Fleet Marmion.*

OCTOBER 28

HOW snugly we slept in my old coat of grey,
And he licked me for kindness- my poor
dog Tray.
CAMPBELL. *Poor Dog Tray.*

OCTOBER 29

HERE rest the relics of a friend below,
Blest with more sense than half the folks I know.
PETER PINDAR
Epitaph to a Spaniel.

OCTOBER 30

NOR last, forget thy faithful dogs.
DRYDEN. *The Uses of the Dog.*

OCTOBER 31

TO all this fame he rose,
Only following his nose.
And, your wonder vain to shorten,
Pointer to Sir John Throckmorton.
COWPER. *A Riddle.*

A FAMOUS COLLEGE PACK.

The Royal Agricultural College at Cirencester has one of the best packs of Beagles in the country. The pack is here seen meeting off after a meet outside the College. The Master leads the pack and the Whips form up on three sides to prevent any breaking away. Individually, somebody's Scotch-kit is hurrying up. The Field follows at a distance.

NOVEMBER

Atheism destroys magnanimity… for, take an example of a dog, and mark what a generosity and courage he will put on when he finds himself maintained by a man, who to him is instead of a God.

BACON.

NOVEMBER 01

I BEGGED old Donald hard- they gave him me-
And we have lived together in this house
Long years, with no companions.
BUCHANAN. *The School Master's Story.*

NOVEMBER 02

HIS strength, his plight, his speed so light,
You had with wonder viewed.
MAGINN. *Argus.*

NOVEMBER 03

DOGS begin in jest and end in earnest.
Old Proverb.

NOVEMBER 04

AND as he grew older
Every beholder
Agreed he grew handsomer, sleeker and bolder.
Ingolsby Legends.

NOVEMBER 05

RESTING his head upon his master's knees,
Upon the bank beside him Theron lay.
What matters change of state and circumstance
to him.
ROBERT SOUTHEY. *Roderick's Faithful Theron.*

NOVEMBER 06

A LOVING creature she brave!
And fondly strives her struggling friend to save.
WORDSWORTH. *Dog's Tragedy.*

NOVEMBER 07

AND till great Snowdon's rocks grow old,
And cease the storm to brave,
The consecrated spot shall hold
The name of "Gelert's Grave!"
SPENSER. *Beth Gelert.*

NOVEMBER 08

THE King therefore he did give every man
Of the best houndis were amoung them.
STEWART. *Battle about a Dog.*

By courtesy of] CHECK BY A HEDGE-ROW. [Dr Jobson-Scott

The Ampleforth College Beagles find the trail end in thin air, probably because, working to leeward of the hare, the intervening hedge has spoilt the scent.

NOVEMBER 09

OF the dog in ancient story
Many a pleasant tale is told.
MARY HOWITT. *Tobias' Dog.*

NOVEMBER 10

THE Proverb old is verified in you;
Love me and love my dog, and so, adieu!
TURBERVILLE. *Love Me, Love my Dog.*

NOVEMBER 11

IN summer's heat he follows by the pace,
In winter's cold he never leaveth thee;
In mountains wild he by thee close doth trace;
In all thy fears and dangers true is he.
MOLLE. *Faithfullest Beast.*

NOVEMBER 12

A WITTY writer of this time
Doth make some mention in a pleasant rhyme
Of Lepidies, and of his famous dog.
HARINGTON. *In praise of Bungey.*

NOVEMBER 13

'TWAS set up above the lave,
The gentle hound was to me slave.
LYNDSAY. *Bagsche's Complaint.*

NOVEMBER 14

COME, Herod, my hound, from stranger's floor!
Old friend, we must wander the world once more!
BARRY CORNWALL. *My Bloodhound.*

NOVEMBER 15

THE dog beside the threshold lies
Mocking sleep, with half shut eyes-
Then quick he pricks his ears to hark,
And bustles up to growl and bark.
CLARKE. *The Guardian.*

NOVEMBER 16

THEN I was a schoolboy, all thoughtless and free,
And thou wert a whelp, full of gambol and glee.
MOIR. Old Oscar.

NOVEMBER 17

UP he sprang in eager haste,
Fawning, fondling, breathing fast
In a tender trouble.
E.B.BROWNING. *To Flush, My dog.*

NOVEMBER 18

THROUGH drifted snow, with ears thrown back,
I'm ready, night or day,
To follow fearless on the track
Of every beast of prey.
MARTIN. *Brave Dog's Challenge.*

NOVEMBER 19

I FEEL a creeping towards me-a soft head-
And on my face
A tender nose, and cold…
That is the way, you know, that dog's embrace.
RAWNSLEY. *We Meet at Morn, my Dog and I.*

NOVEMBER 20

I BOUGHT a dog- a queen!
Ah, Tiny dear departing pug!
She lives, but she is past sixteen.
CALVERLEY. *Disasters.*

[Photo] BE CAREFUL. [Furien Leigh.

There is much unintentional cruelty to animals and many a puppy is cowed by the over-affectionate child who is inclined to crush its new pet, causing it pain and, occasionally, injury. Children should be taught not to play with puppies, but to allow puppies to play with them—there's a difference.

NOVEMBER 21

NOW beat the hound no more!
Give o'er thy cruel blows, he cried; a man's soul verily
Is lodged in that same crouching beast.
SIR E. ARNOLD. *The Pythagorean.*

NOVEMBER 22

DAY after day I have come and sat
Beseechingly upon the mat,
Wistfully wondering what you are at!
MASSEY. *Dead Boy's Portrait.*

NOVEMBER 23

DEAR little friend, who, day by day,
Before the door of home,
Art ready waiting till thy master come.
LEWIS MORRIS. *To the Tormentors.*

NOVEMBER 24

WHY should not a dog have a soul like any other respectable Christian?
Buchanan to G. Lewis.
I ONCE had a sheep-dog for guide.
HOOD. *Lament of a Poor Blind.*

NOVEMBER 25

AN hunde there was beside
That was yclep Hodain,
Togider thai gun abide
In joy and ek in pain.
THOMAS THE RHYMER, 1226

NOVEMBER 26

GO, like the Indian, in another life,
Expect thy dog, thy bottle, and thy wife,
An Essay on Man, Epis. iv.

NOVEMBER 27

THE dame made a curtsey,
The dog made a bow;
The dame said, "Your servant,"
The dog said, "Bow-wow."
UINKNOWN.

NOVEMBER 28

THE fleetest hound in all the north-
Brave Lufra saw, and darted forth.
SCOTT. *Lufra Avenged.*

NOVEMBER 29

THE royal hunter his brave hound caressed,
Launded his zeal and spirit unsubdued.
HOGG. *The Deep-Toned Jowler.*

NOVEMBER 30

FEW, at the date, arrive of ancient Argus,
Kind, sagacious brute!
Not e'en Minerva's wisdom could conceal
Thy much-loved master from thy nicer sense.
SOMERVILLE. *The chase.*

NOTES

THE BEAGLE A " REYNALTON " PUPPY

DECEMBER

...Mine is no narrow creed;
And He how gave thee being did not frame
The mystery of life, to be the sport
Of merciless man! There is another world
For all that live and move- a better one!
Where the proud bipeds, who would fain confine
Infinite goodness to the little bounds
Of their own charity, may envy thee.

ROBERT SOUTHEY.
Canine Immortality.

DECEMBER 01

AND now, with many a frisk,
Wide scampering, snatches up the drifted snow
With ivory teeth, or ploughs it with his snout,
Then shakes his powdered coat, and barks for joy.
COWPER. *The Task*.

DECEMBER 02

OFT listening how the hounds and horn
Cheerily rose the slumbering morn,
From the side of some hoar hill
Through the high wood echoing shrill.
MILTON. *L'Allegro*.

DECEMBER 03

I COULDN'T have any other dog but Jip; it would be so unkind to Jip.
DICKENS. *David Copperfield*.

DECEMBER 04

BLESSINGS on thee, dog of mine.
… Hands of gentle motion fail
Nevermore to pat thee!
E.B BROWNING. *To Flush, my Dog*.

DECEMBER 05

NO joy did divide us; no peril could part
The man from his friend of the noble heart.
BARRY CORNWALL. *My Bloodhound.*

DECEMBER 06

AN' e sarved me so well when 'e lived, that when
'e comes to be deäd,
I thinks as I'd like fur to have some soort o' a
sarvice reaä.
TENNYSON. *Owd Roä.*

DECEMBER 07

THOUGH solitude around is spread,
Master, alone thou shalt not be.
BOWLES. *Grown Old Together.*

A MATE how dear.
MATTHEW ARNOLD. *Kaiser Dead.*

DECEMBER 08

NOT long after Tray did the shepherd remain,
…Oh, bury me, neighbours, beside my old
friend.
PETER PINDAR. *Old Friends.*

EVEN pearls are dark before the whiteness of his
teeth.
ALGER. *Charity's Eyes.*

THE BEAGLE
CH. RANTER OF REYNALTON
CH. MELODY OF REYNALTON

DECEMBER 09

BETTER dog one wouldn't wish for in his way.
HORSFIELD. *Old Rocket.*

SELECT a few, and form them by degrees
To stricter discipline.
SOMERVILLE. *The Chase.*

DECEMBER 10

THIS dog hath so himself subdued,
… And his behaviour does confess
True courage dwells with gentleness.
KATHERINE PHILLIPS. *The Trick Greyhound.*

DECEMBER 11

NOW, Pilos, see how mannerly your cur,
Yon well-taught dog, that hath so many tricks.
BROWNE. *A Comedy.*

DECEMBER 12

I AM misanthropos, and hate mankind.
For my part, I do wish thou wert a dog
That I might love thee.
SHAKESPEARE. *Timon of Athens, iv 3*

DECEMBER 13

TO please but thee he spareth for no pains,
His hurt (for thee) is greatest good to him.
MOLLE. *The Faithfullest Beast.*

DECEMBER 14

HE growled in anger, and in love caressed,
No human falsehood lurked beneath his heart;
Brave without boasting, generous without art.
UNKNOWN. *Lord Orrery's Hector.*

DECEMBER 15

EHEU! Hic jacet Crony,
A dog of much renown,
Nec fur, nec macaroni,
Though born and bed in town.
UNKNOWN. *Dog Latin.*

DECEMBER 16

YET hath not Jockie, nor yet Willie, seen a dog
more nimble than is this of mine.
BROWNE. *A Comedy.*

DECEMBER 17

IN fields abroad he looks unto thy flocks,
Keeping them safe from wolves and other beasts.
MOLLE. *The Faithfullest Beast.*

DECEMBER 18

SIX years ago I brought him down
A baby dog, from London town;
Round his small throat of black and brown
A ribbon blue.
MATTHEW ARNOLD. *Kaiser.*

DECEMBER 19

… YET here at nights I sit
Reading the Book, with Donald at my side;
I sometimes gaze in Donald's patient eyes,
So sad, so human, though he cannot speak.
BUCHANAN. *The Schoolmaster's Story.*

DECEMBER 20

MOST beloved of masters, pray don't go to bed;
You had much better sit up and pat me instead!
BARHAM. *Sancho, the Bagman's Dog.*

THE BEAGLE　　　　　　　　　　Ch. Ranter of Reynalton

DECEMBER 21

AND as he is thy faithful bodyguard,
So he is good within a fort or hold
Against a quick surprise to watch and ward.
MOLLE.

DECEMBER 22

THE king a welp he brought
Bifor Tristrem the trewe;
… Silke was non so soft;
He was red, grene, and blewe.
THOMAS THE RHYMER, 1226

DECEMBER 23

MY name came first from Holy Hubert's race,
Soygllard, my sire, a hound of singular grace.
JAQUES DU FOUILLOUX.

THE best dog in the east-nook coast.
HAMILTON. *Bonny Heck.*

DECEMBER 24

THE greyhound; the great hound! The graceful
of limb!
Rough fellow! Tall fellow! Swift fellow, and
slim!
An old MS.

DECEMBER 25

WE country dogs love noble sport,
And scorn the pranks of dogs at court.
UNKNOWN. *Bounce to Top.*

A VERY plain and downright honest dog.
HAMILTON. *The Dog Incog.*

DECEMBER 26

IN sooth he was a peerless hound,
The gift of royal John.
SPENSER. *Beth Gelert.*

THE best of all friends.
BARRY CORNWALL. *My Bloodhound.*

DECEMBER 27

I WONDER who'll have yer, my beauty,
When him as you're all to's dead.
SIMS *Told to the Missionary.*

ILKA dog has his day, O.
MACLEOD.

DECEMBER 28

OBEDIENCE to a master's will
Had taught the dog to roam,
And through the terrors of the waste
To fetch the wanderer home.
CAROLINE FRY. *The Dog of St. Bernard's*

DECEMBER 29

COULD well understand
The word of command,
And appear to doze
With a crust on his nose...
As he sat up on end on his little cocktail.
BARHAM. *Sancho.*

DECEMBER 30

HE meant to have helped him again,
Thereto he did all his main,
Great kindness is in houndis!
Mediaval Romance, ii

DECEMBER 31

IT is not from unwillingness to praise,
Or want of love, that here no stone we raise;
More thou deservest,
But *this* man gives to man,
Brother to brother, this is all we can
Get, they to whom thy virtues made thee dear
Shall find thee through all changes of the year.
WORDSWORTH.

2011

January
Su	Mo	Tu	We	Th	Fr	Sa
						1
2	3	4	5	6	7	8
9	10	11	12	13	14	15
16	17	18	19	20	21	22
23	24	25	26	27	28	29
30	31					

February
Su	Mo	Tu	We	Th	Fr	Sa
		1	2	3	4	5
6	7	8	9	10	11	12
13	14	15	16	17	18	19
20	21	22	23	24	25	26
27	28					

March
Su	Mo	Tu	We	Th	Fr	Sa
		1	2	3	4	5
6	7	8	9	10	11	12
13	14	15	16	17	18	19
20	21	22	23	24	25	26
27	28	29	30	31		

April
Su	Mo	Tu	We	Th	Fr	Sa
					1	2
3	4	5	6	7	8	9
10	11	12	13	14	15	16
17	18	19	20	21	22	23
24	25	26	27	28	29	30

May
Su	Mo	Tu	We	Th	Fr	Sa
1	2	3	4	5	6	7
8	9	10	11	12	13	14
15	16	17	18	19	20	21
22	23	24	25	26	27	28
29	30	31				

June
Su	Mo	Tu	We	Th	Fr	Sa
			1	2	3	4
5	6	7	8	9	10	11
12	13	14	15	16	17	18
19	20	21	22	23	24	25
26	27	28	29	30		

July
Su	Mo	Tu	We	Th	Fr	Sa
					1	2
3	4	5	6	7	8	9
10	11	12	13	14	15	16
17	18	19	20	21	22	23
24	25	26	27	28	29	30
31						

August
Su	Mo	Tu	We	Th	Fr	Sa
	1	2	3	4	5	6
7	8	9	10	11	12	13
14	15	16	17	18	19	20
21	22	23	24	25	26	27
28	29	30	31			

September
Su	Mo	Tu	We	Th	Fr	Sa
				1	2	3
4	5	6	7	8	9	10
11	12	13	14	15	16	17
18	19	20	21	22	23	24
25	26	27	28	29	30	

October
Su	Mo	Tu	We	Th	Fr	Sa
						1
2	3	4	5	6	7	8
9	10	11	12	13	14	15
16	17	18	19	20	21	22
23	24	25	26	27	28	29
30	31					

November
Su	Mo	Tu	We	Th	Fr	Sa
		1	2	3	4	5
6	7	8	9	10	11	12
13	14	15	16	17	18	19
20	21	22	23	24	25	26
27	28	29	30			

December
Su	Mo	Tu	We	Th	Fr	Sa
				1	2	3
4	5	6	7	8	9	10
11	12	13	14	15	16	17
18	19	20	21	22	23	24
25	26	27	28	29	30	31

2012

January
Su	Mo	Tu	We	Th	Fr	Sa
1	2	3	4	5	6	7
8	9	10	11	12	13	14
15	16	17	18	19	20	21
22	23	24	25	26	27	28
29	30	31				

February
Su	Mo	Tu	We	Th	Fr	Sa
			1	2	3	4
5	6	7	8	9	10	11
12	13	14	15	16	17	18
19	20	21	22	23	24	25
26	27	28	29			

March
Su	Mo	Tu	We	Th	Fr	Sa
				1	2	3
4	5	6	7	8	9	10
11	12	13	14	15	16	17
18	19	20	21	22	23	24
25	26	27	28	29	30	31

April
Su	Mo	Tu	We	Th	Fr	Sa
1	2	3	4	5	6	7
8	9	10	11	12	13	14
15	16	17	18	19	20	21
22	23	24	25	26	27	28
29	30					

May
Su	Mo	Tu	We	Th	Fr	Sa
		1	2	3	4	5
6	7	8	9	10	11	12
13	14	15	16	17	18	19
20	21	22	23	24	25	26
27	28	29	30	31		

June
Su	Mo	Tu	We	Th	Fr	Sa
					1	2
3	4	5	6	7	8	9
10	11	12	13	14	15	16
17	18	19	20	21	22	23
24	25	26	27	28	29	30

July
Su	Mo	Tu	We	Th	Fr	Sa
1	2	3	4	5	6	7
8	9	10	11	12	13	14
15	16	17	18	19	20	21
22	23	24	25	26	27	28
29	30	31				

August
Su	Mo	Tu	We	Th	Fr	Sa
			1	2	3	4
5	6	7	8	9	10	11
12	13	14	15	16	17	18
19	20	21	22	23	24	25
26	27	28	29	30	31	

September
Su	Mo	Tu	We	Th	Fr	Sa
						1
2	3	4	5	6	7	8
9	10	11	12	13	14	15
16	17	18	19	20	21	22
23	24	25	26	27	28	29
30						

October
Su	Mo	Tu	We	Th	Fr	Sa
	1	2	3	4	5	6
7	8	9	10	11	12	13
14	15	16	17	18	19	20
21	22	23	24	25	26	27
28	29	30	31			

November
Su	Mo	Tu	We	Th	Fr	Sa
				1	2	3
4	5	6	7	8	9	10
11	12	13	14	15	16	17
18	19	20	21	22	23	24
25	26	27	28	29	30	

December
Su	Mo	Tu	We	Th	Fr	Sa
						1
2	3	4	5	6	7	8
9	10	11	12	13	14	15
16	17	18	19	20	21	22
23	24	25	26	27	28	29
30	31					

2014

January
Su	Mo	Tu	We	Th	Fr	Sa
			1	2	3	4
5	6	7	8	9	10	11
12	13	14	15	16	17	18
19	20	21	22	23	24	25
26	27	28	29	30	31	

February
Su	Mo	Tu	We	Th	Fr	Sa
						1
2	3	4	5	6	7	8
9	10	11	12	13	14	15
16	17	18	19	20	21	22
23	24	25	26	27	28	

March
Su	Mo	Tu	We	Th	Fr	Sa
						1
2	3	4	5	6	7	8
9	10	11	12	13	14	15
16	17	18	19	20	21	22
23	24	25	26	27	28	29
30	31					

April
Su	Mo	Tu	We	Th	Fr	Sa
		1	2	3	4	5
6	7	8	9	10	11	12
13	14	15	16	17	18	19
20	21	22	23	24	25	26
27	28	29	30			

May
Su	Mo	Tu	We	Th	Fr	Sa
				1	2	3
4	5	6	7	8	9	10
11	12	13	14	15	16	17
18	19	20	21	22	23	24
25	26	27	28	29	30	31

June
Su	Mo	Tu	We	Th	Fr	Sa
1	2	3	4	5	6	7
8	9	10	11	12	13	14
15	16	17	18	19	20	21
22	23	24	25	26	27	28
29	30					

July
Su	Mo	Tu	We	Th	Fr	Sa
		1	2	3	4	5
6	7	8	9	10	11	12
13	14	15	16	17	18	19
20	21	22	23	24	25	26
27	28	29	30	31		

August
Su	Mo	Tu	We	Th	Fr	Sa
					1	2
3	4	5	6	7	8	9
10	11	12	13	14	15	16
17	18	19	20	21	22	23
24	25	26	27	28	29	30
31						

September
Su	Mo	Tu	We	Th	Fr	Sa
	1	2	3	4	5	6
7	8	9	10	11	12	13
14	15	16	17	18	19	20
21	22	23	24	25	26	27
28	29	30				

October
Su	Mo	Tu	We	Th	Fr	Sa
			1	2	3	4
5	6	7	8	9	10	11
12	13	14	15	16	17	18
19	20	21	22	23	24	25
26	27	28	29	30	31	

November
Su	Mo	Tu	We	Th	Fr	Sa
						1
2	3	4	5	6	7	8
9	10	11	12	13	14	15
16	17	18	19	20	21	22
23	24	25	26	27	28	29
30						

December
Su	Mo	Tu	We	Th	Fr	Sa
	1	2	3	4	5	6
7	8	9	10	11	12	13
14	15	16	17	18	19	20
21	22	23	24	25	26	27
28	29	30	31			

2013

January
Su	Mo	Tu	We	Th	Fr	Sa
		1	2	3	4	5
6	7	8	9	10	11	12
13	14	15	16	17	18	19
20	21	22	23	24	25	26
27	28	29	30	31		

February
Su	Mo	Tu	We	Th	Fr	Sa
					1	2
3	4	5	6	7	8	9
10	11	12	13	14	15	16
17	18	19	20	21	22	23
24	25	26	27	28		

March
Su	Mo	Tu	We	Th	Fr	Sa
					1	2
3	4	5	6	7	8	9
10	11	12	13	14	15	16
17	18	19	20	21	22	23
24	25	26	27	28	29	30
31						

April
Su	Mo	Tu	We	Th	Fr	Sa
	1	2	3	4	5	6
7	8	9	10	11	12	13
14	15	16	17	18	19	20
21	22	23	24	25	26	27
28	29	30				

May
Su	Mo	Tu	We	Th	Fr	Sa
			1	2	3	4
5	6	7	8	9	10	11
12	13	14	15	16	17	18
19	20	21	22	23	24	25
26	27	28	29	30	31	

June
Su	Mo	Tu	We	Th	Fr	Sa
						1
2	3	4	5	6	7	8
9	10	11	12	13	14	15
16	17	18	19	20	21	22
23	24	25	26	27	28	29
30						

July
Su	Mo	Tu	We	Th	Fr	Sa
	1	2	3	4	5	6
7	8	9	10	11	12	13
14	15	16	17	18	19	20
21	22	23	24	25	26	27
28	29	30	31			

August
Su	Mo	Tu	We	Th	Fr	Sa
				1	2	3
4	5	6	7	8	9	10
11	12	13	14	15	16	17
18	19	20	21	22	23	24
25	26	27	28	29	30	31

September
Su	Mo	Tu	We	Th	Fr	Sa
1	2	3	4	5	6	7
8	9	10	11	12	13	14
15	16	17	18	19	20	21
22	23	24	25	26	27	28
29	30					

October
Su	Mo	Tu	We	Th	Fr	Sa
		1	2	3	4	5
6	7	8	9	10	11	12
13	14	15	16	17	18	19
20	21	22	23	24	25	26
27	28	29	30	31		

November
Su	Mo	Tu	We	Th	Fr	Sa
					1	2
3	4	5	6	7	8	9
10	11	12	13	14	15	16
17	18	19	20	21	22	23
24	25	26	27	28	29	30

December
Su	Mo	Tu	We	Th	Fr	Sa
1	2	3	4	5	6	7
8	9	10	11	12	13	14
15	16	17	18	19	20	21
22	23	24	25	26	27	28
29	30	31				

2018

January
Su	Mo	Tu	We	Th	Fr	Sa
	1	2	3	4	5	6
7	8	9	10	11	12	13
14	15	16	17	18	19	20
21	22	23	24	25	26	27
28	29	30	31			

February
Su	Mo	Tu	We	Th	Fr	Sa
				1	2	3
4	5	6	7	8	9	10
11	12	13	14	15	16	17
18	19	20	21	22	23	24
25	26	27	28			

March
Su	Mo	Tu	We	Th	Fr	Sa
				1	2	3
4	5	6	7	8	9	10
11	12	13	14	15	16	17
18	19	20	21	22	23	24
25	26	27	28	29	30	31

April
Su	Mo	Tu	We	Th	Fr	Sa
1	2	3	4	5	6	7
8	9	10	11	12	13	14
15	16	17	18	19	20	21
22	23	24	25	26	27	28
29	30					

May
Su	Mo	Tu	We	Th	Fr	Sa
		1	2	3	4	5
6	7	8	9	10	11	12
13	14	15	16	17	18	19
20	21	22	23	24	25	26
27	28	29	30	31		

June
Su	Mo	Tu	We	Th	Fr	Sa
					1	2
3	4	5	6	7	8	9
10	11	12	13	14	15	16
17	18	19	20	21	22	23
24	25	26	27	28	29	30

July
Su	Mo	Tu	We	Th	Fr	Sa
1	2	3	4	5	6	7
8	9	10	11	12	13	14
15	16	17	18	19	20	21
22	23	24	25	26	27	28
29	30	31				

August
Su	Mo	Tu	We	Th	Fr	Sa
			1	2	3	4
5	6	7	8	9	10	11
12	13	14	15	16	17	18
19	20	21	22	23	24	25
26	27	28	29	30	31	

September
Su	Mo	Tu	We	Th	Fr	Sa
						1
2	3	4	5	6	7	8
9	10	11	12	13	14	15
16	17	18	19	20	21	22
23	24	25	26	27	28	29
30						

October
Su	Mo	Tu	We	Th	Fr	Sa
	1	2	3	4	5	6
7	8	9	10	11	12	13
14	15	16	17	18	19	20
21	22	23	24	25	26	27
28	29	30	31			

November
Su	Mo	Tu	We	Th	Fr	Sa
				1	2	3
4	5	6	7	8	9	10
11	12	13	14	15	16	17
18	19	20	21	22	23	24
25	26	27	28	29	30	

December
Su	Mo	Tu	We	Th	Fr	Sa
						1
2	3	4	5	6	7	8
9	10	11	12	13	14	15
16	17	18	19	20	21	22
23	24	25	26	27	28	29
30	31					

2017

January
Su	Mo	Tu	We	Th	Fr	Sa
1	2	3	4	5	6	7
8	9	10	11	12	13	14
15	16	17	18	19	20	21
22	23	24	25	26	27	28
29	30	31				

February
Su	Mo	Tu	We	Th	Fr	Sa
			1	2	3	4
5	6	7	8	9	10	11
12	13	14	15	16	17	18
19	20	21	22	23	24	25
26	27	28				

March
Su	Mo	Tu	We	Th	Fr	Sa
			1	2	3	4
5	6	7	8	9	10	11
12	13	14	15	16	17	18
19	20	21	22	23	24	25
26	27	28	29	30	31	

April
Su	Mo	Tu	We	Th	Fr	Sa
						1
2	3	4	5	6	7	8
9	10	11	12	13	14	15
16	17	18	19	20	21	22
23	24	25	26	27	28	29
30						

May
Su	Mo	Tu	We	Th	Fr	Sa
	1	2	3	4	5	6
7	8	9	10	11	12	13
14	15	16	17	18	19	20
21	22	23	24	25	26	27
28	29	30	31			

June
Su	Mo	Tu	We	Th	Fr	Sa
				1	2	3
4	5	6	7	8	9	10
11	12	13	14	15	16	17
18	19	20	21	22	23	24
25	26	27	28	29	30	

July
Su	Mo	Tu	We	Th	Fr	Sa
						1
2	3	4	5	6	7	8
9	10	11	12	13	14	15
16	17	18	19	20	21	22
23	24	25	26	27	28	29
30	31					

August
Su	Mo	Tu	We	Th	Fr	Sa
		1	2	3	4	5
6	7	8	9	10	11	12
13	14	15	16	17	18	19
20	21	22	23	24	25	26
27	28	29	30	31		

September
Su	Mo	Tu	We	Th	Fr	Sa
					1	2
3	4	5	6	7	8	9
10	11	12	13	14	15	16
17	18	19	20	21	22	23
24	25	26	27	28	29	30

October
Su	Mo	Tu	We	Th	Fr	Sa
1	2	3	4	5	6	7
8	9	10	11	12	13	14
15	16	17	18	19	20	21
22	23	24	25	26	27	28
29	30	31				

November
Su	Mo	Tu	We	Th	Fr	Sa
			1	2	3	4
5	6	7	8	9	10	11
12	13	14	15	16	17	18
19	20	21	22	23	24	25
26	27	28	29	30		

December
Su	Mo	Tu	We	Th	Fr	Sa
					1	2
3	4	5	6	7	8	9
10	11	12	13	14	15	16
17	18	19	20	21	22	23
24	25	26	27	28	29	30
31						

2015

January
Su	Mo	Tu	We	Th	Fr	Sa
				1	2	3
4	5	6	7	8	9	10
11	12	13	14	15	16	17
18	19	20	21	22	23	24
25	26	27	28	29	30	31

February
Su	Mo	Tu	We	Th	Fr	Sa
1	2	3	4	5	6	7
8	9	10	11	12	13	14
15	16	17	18	19	20	21
22	23	24	25	26	27	28

March
Su	Mo	Tu	We	Th	Fr	Sa
1	2	3	4	5	6	7
8	9	10	11	12	13	14
15	16	17	18	19	20	21
22	23	24	25	26	27	28
29	30	31				

April
Su	Mo	Tu	We	Th	Fr	Sa
			1	2	3	4
5	6	7	8	9	10	11
12	13	14	15	16	17	18
19	20	21	22	23	24	25
26	27	28	29	30		

May
Su	Mo	Tu	We	Th	Fr	Sa
					1	2
3	4	5	6	7	8	9
10	11	12	13	14	15	16
17	18	19	20	21	22	23
24	25	26	27	28	29	30
31						

June
Su	Mo	Tu	We	Th	Fr	Sa
	1	2	3	4	5	6
7	8	9	10	11	12	13
14	15	16	17	18	19	20
21	22	23	24	25	26	27
28	29	30				

July
Su	Mo	Tu	We	Th	Fr	Sa
			1	2	3	4
5	6	7	8	9	10	11
12	13	14	15	16	17	18
19	20	21	22	23	24	25
26	27	28	29	30	31	

August
Su	Mo	Tu	We	Th	Fr	Sa
						1
2	3	4	5	6	7	8
9	10	11	12	13	14	15
16	17	18	19	20	21	22
23	24	25	26	27	28	29
30	31					

September
Su	Mo	Tu	We	Th	Fr	Sa
		1	2	3	4	5
6	7	8	9	10	11	12
13	14	15	16	17	18	19
20	21	22	23	24	25	26
27	28	29	30			

October
Su	Mo	Tu	We	Th	Fr	Sa
				1	2	3
4	5	6	7	8	9	10
11	12	13	14	15	16	17
18	19	20	21	22	23	24
25	26	27	28	29	30	31

November
Su	Mo	Tu	We	Th	Fr	Sa
1	2	3	4	5	6	7
8	9	10	11	12	13	14
15	16	17	18	19	20	21
22	23	24	25	26	27	28
29	30					

December
Su	Mo	Tu	We	Th	Fr	Sa
		1	2	3	4	5
6	7	8	9	10	11	12
13	14	15	16	17	18	19
20	21	22	23	24	25	26
27	28	29	30	31		

Material in this book has been sourced from the following titles:

J. H. Walsh. *The Dogs Of The British Islands*. 1867
Vero Shaw. *The Illustrated Book Of The Dog*. 1879
Rawdon B. Lee. *A History And Description Of The Modern Dogs*. 1894
H. W. Huntington. *My Dog And I*. 1897
H. W. Huntington. *The Show Dog*. 1901
C. H. Lane. *Dog Shows And Doggy People*. 1902
W, D. Drury. *British Dogs - Their Points, Selection, And Show Preparation*. 1903
Frank Townend Barton. *Sporting Dogs - Their Points: And Management*. 1905
James Watson. *The Dog Book - A Popular History Of The Dog*. 1906
J. Sidney Turner. *The Kennel Encyclopaedia*. 1907
Frank Townend Barton. *Hounds*. 1913
A. Croxton Smith. *About Our Dogs - The Breeds And Their Management*. 1931
Walter Hutchinson. *Hutchinson's Dog Encyclopaedia*. 1935
Stanley West. *The Book Of Dogs*. 1935
Francis Butler. *Breeding, Training, Management, Diseases, Etc*. 1857
Robert Kaleski. *Australian Barkers And Biters*. 1914
Arthur Craven. *Dogs Of The World*. 1931
Various. *The Beagle Hound - A Complete Anthology Of The Dog*. 2010

Lightning Source UK Ltd.
Milton Keynes UK
UKOW050323280212

188032UK00004B/2/P

9 781447 427766